MW01627109

With Love:

Mom, I Love You Always and Forever

Designed by Christian Art Gifts

Images used under license from Shutterstock.com

Printed in China

ISBN 978-1-4321-1811-2

Christian Art Gifts has made every effort to trace the ownership of all quotes and poems in this book. In the event of any question that may arise from the use of any quote or poem, we regret any error made and will be pleased to make the necessary correction in future editions of this book.

18 19 20 21 22 23 24 25 26 27 – 11 10 9 8 7 6 5 4 3 2

MOM, I LOVE YOU *always and forever*

AMAZING
LOVING
STRONG
HAPPY
SELFLESS
GRACEFUL

SHE IS WORTH
FAR MORE
THAN Rubies
PROVERBS 31:10

A Mother is your first friend your best friend your forever friend

A friend loves at all times
Proverbs 17:17

It is well with my soul.

Horatio G. Spafford

Happy are the people whose God is the Lord!

Psalm 144:15

I love
the little
things
you do!

Whatever your hand
finds to do,
do it with all your might.
Ecclesiastes 9:10

plant smiles • grow laughter • harvest love

Blessed
is the one whose delight
is in the Lord. That person is like
a tree planted by streams of water ...
whatever they do prospers.
PSALM 1:1-3

All that
I am or
ever hope to be,
I owe to my
angel mother.

Abraham Lincoln

She
speaks with
wisdom & faithful
instruction is on
her tongue.
Proverbs 31:26

Every good
and perfect gift
is from above,
coming down from
the Father of the
heavenly lights.
James 1:17

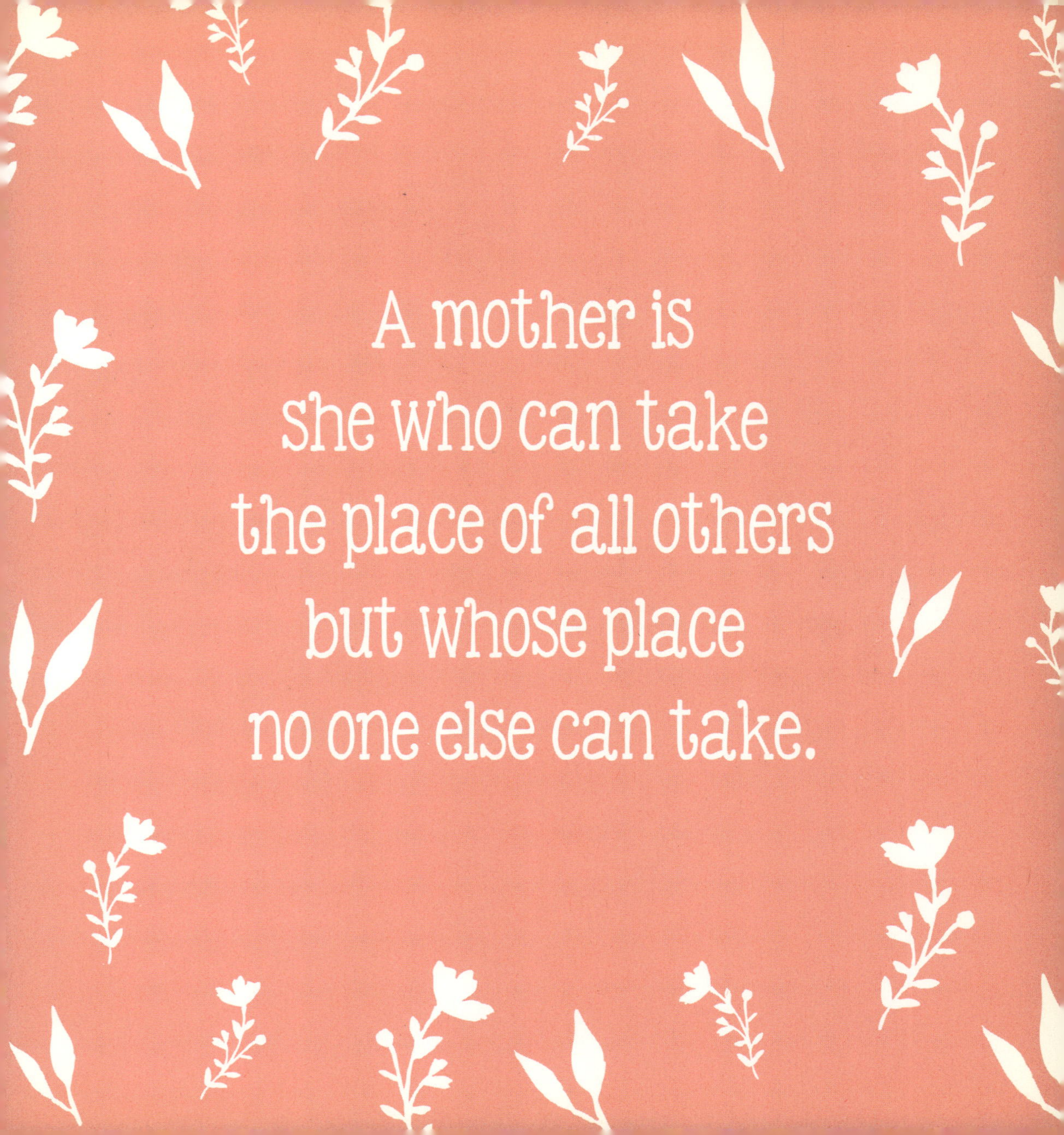
A mother is
she who can take
the place of all others
but whose place
no one else can take.

These three remain: faith, hope and love. But the greatest of these is love.

1 Corinthians 13:13

A mother's
heart
IS A
patchwork
OF
love

Family
is a little world
created by a mother's love.

By wisdom a house is built,
and through understanding it is established;
through knowledge its rooms are filled
with rare and beautiful treasures.

Proverbs 24:3-4

A MOTHER'S ARMS
ARE MADE OF
tenderness
AND CHILDREN SLEEP
SOUNDLY IN THEM.

I sleep and wake up refreshed
because You, LORD,
protect me.
Psalm 3:5

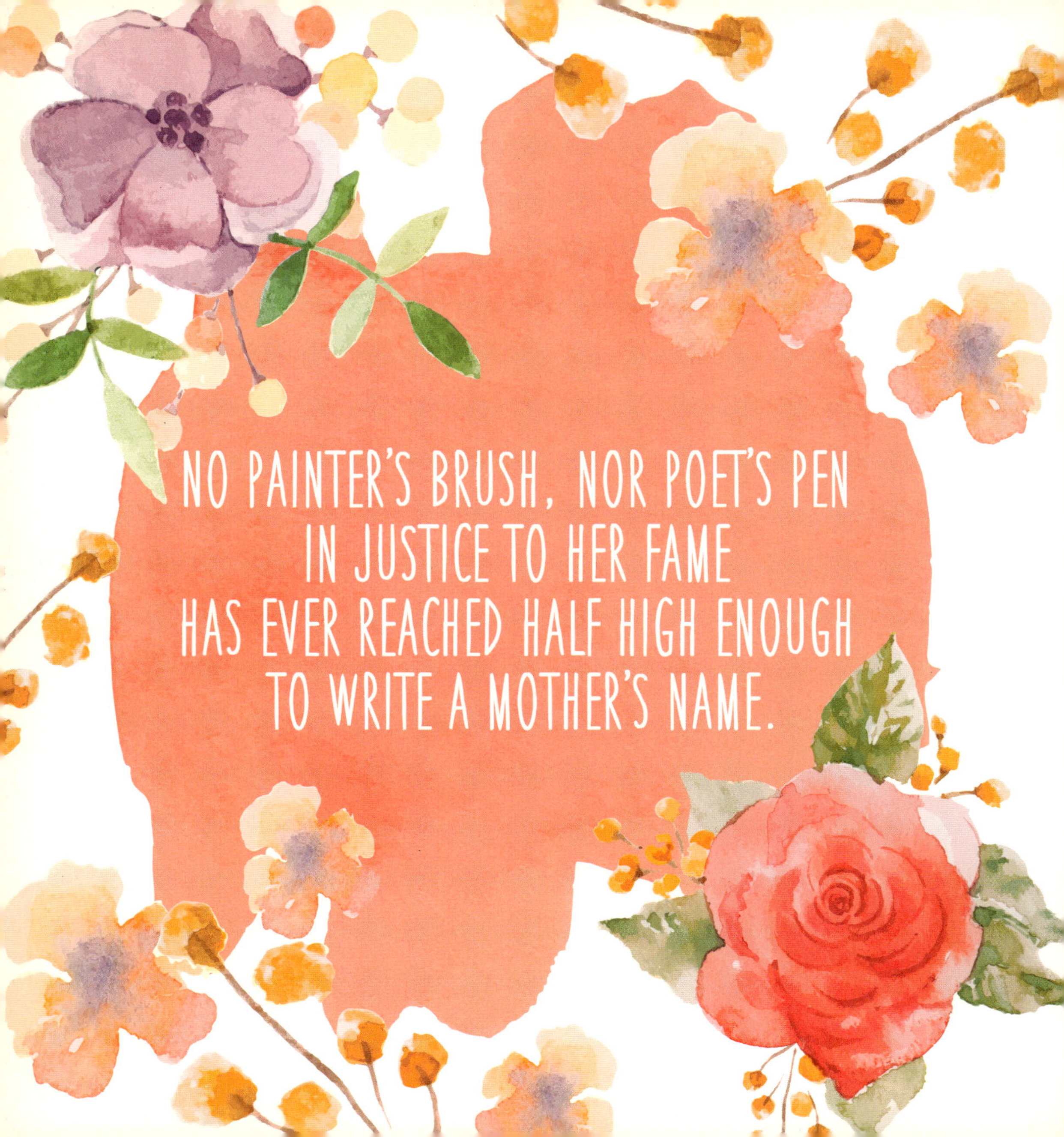
NO PAINTER'S BRUSH, NOR POET'S PEN
IN JUSTICE TO HER FAME
HAS EVER REACHED HALF HIGH ENOUGH
TO WRITE A MOTHER'S NAME.

Honor her
for all that her
hands have done,
and let her works
bring her praise.

PROVERBS 31:31

Faith
makes the impossible possible.

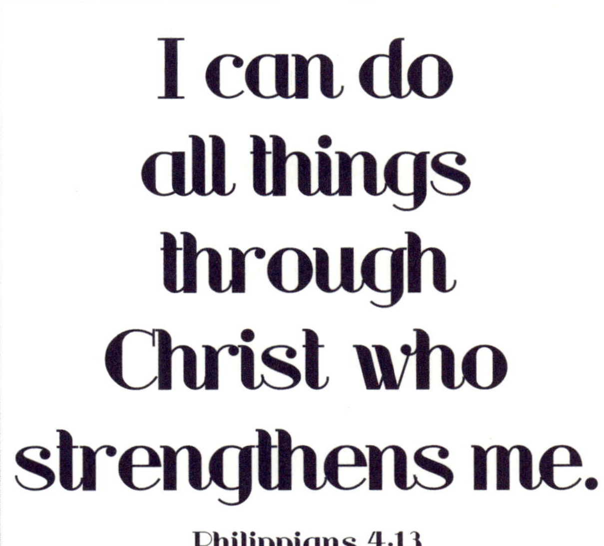
I can do
all things
through
Christ who
strengthens me.
Philippians 4:13

A mother strengthens her children with prayer, encourages them with hope and blesses them with love.

We are God's masterpiece.

Ephesians 2:10

Mom,
our nest is blessed
because of you!

God will cover you with His *feathers*

He will shelter you with His wings.

Psalm 91:4

Grow in the grace and knowledge of our Lord and Savior Jesus Christ. To Him be glory both now and forever!

2 Peter 3:18

Always my mother
forever my friend.

Start children off on the way they should go, and even when they are old they will not turn from it.

Proverbs 22:6

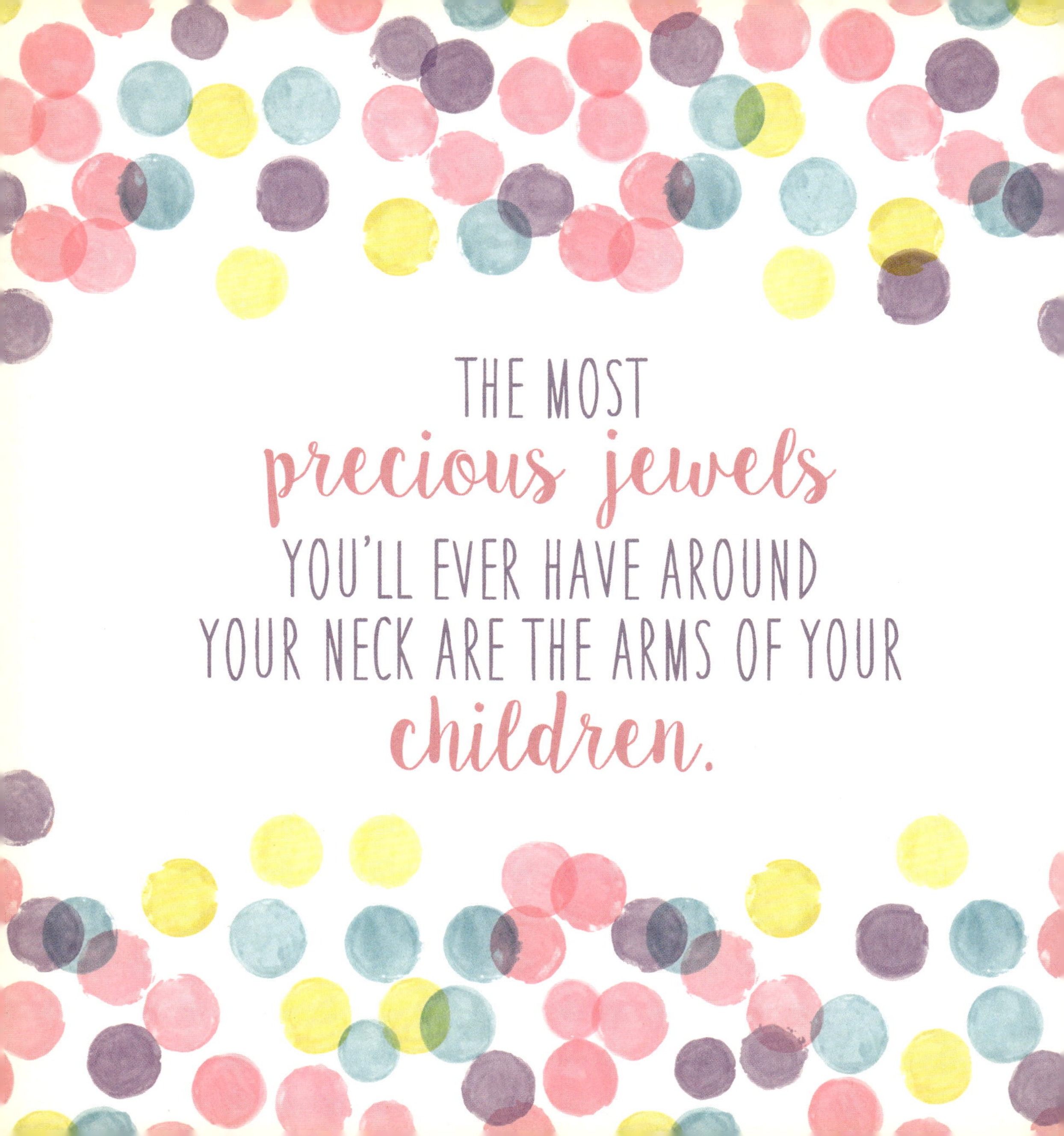
THE MOST
precious jewels
YOU'LL EVER HAVE AROUND
YOUR NECK ARE THE ARMS OF YOUR
children.

Love each other deeply.

1 PETER 4:8

"NEVER WILL I LEAVE YOU; NEVER WILL I FORSAKE YOU."
HEBREWS 13:5

As a mother
my job is to
take care of the
POSSIBLE
and
TRUST GOD
with the impossible.
RUTH BELL GRAHAM

Faith makes all things possible.
Love makes all things easy.
Hope makes all things work.

What is a MOM but the *sunshine* of our days

and the *north star* of our nights.

A mother's arms are made of tenderness and children sleep soundly in them.

I pray that God will greatly
bless you with kindness,
peace and love!

Jude 2

Children are a gift from the Lord; they are a reward from Him.

Psalm 127:3

Motherhood
is the gift
of God to
women.
Mother Teresa